How to Take the GRRRR Out of Anger

Elizabeth Verdick
& Marjorie Lisovskis

Illustrated by Steve Mark

free spirit
PUBLISHING®

Text copyright © 2015, 2003 by Elizabeth Verdick and Marjorie Lisovskis
Illustrations copyright © 2015 by Free Spirit Publishing Inc.

Library of Congress Cataloging-in-Publication Data
Verdick, Elizabeth.
  How to take the grrrr out of anger / by Elizabeth Verdick & Marjorie Lisovskis. — Revised and updated edition
       pages cm. — (Laugh & learn series)
    Includes index.
      ISBN 978-1-57542-494-1 (paperback) — ISBN 1-57542-494-0 (paperback) 1. Anger in children—Juvenile literature. I. Lisovskis, Marjorie. II. Title.
    BF723.A4V47 2015
    152.4'7—dc23
                                                                                2014037076
ISBN: 978-1-57542-494-1

"Relax in 10 Easy Steps" (pages 17–18) is reprinted from *Stress Can Really Get on Your Nerves!* by Trevor Romain and Elizabeth Verdick (Minneapolis: Free Spirit Publishing, 2000), pp. 76–77. Used with permission.

Reading Level Grade 4; Interest Level Ages 8–13;
Fountas & Pinnell Guided Reading Level Q

Cover and interior design by Michelle Lee Lagerroos
Illustrations by Steve Mark

10 9 8 7 6 5 4
Printed in China
R18861217

Free Spirit Publishing Inc.
6325 Sandburg Road, Suite 100
Minneapolis, MN 55427-3674
(612) 338-2068
help4kids@freespirit.com
www.freespirit.com

Sincere thanks to:

All the adults and kids who shared ideas, anecdotes, inspiration, and wisdom as we wrote the book.

The child development specialists, teachers, parents, and grandparents who read the manuscript for the original edition and offered expertise, including Karen Ireland Dahlen; Vian Gredvig, M.S.W., L.I.C.S.W.; Thomas S. Greenspon, Ph.D.; Alice Hansbarger, M.Ed.; Bob Schwalm; and Cady Schwalm.

Psychologist James J. Crist, Ph.D., who reviewed the manuscript for the revised and updated edition and contributed many helpful suggestions.

Contents

Introduction

Why You Need This Book

Everyone gets angry. There isn't one person on the planet who hasn't been angry before. Some people deal with their anger a lot better than others. And some can't seem to cope with their anger at all.

No matter who you are, anger can make you feel like a real monster.

When you're angry, your mind and body may react in these "monstrous" ways:

- **Your brain races with terrible thoughts**
- You want to yell, scream, or shout
- **You grit your teeth**
- You scowl at people
- **Your hands ball up into fists**
- Your heart pounds
- **Your stomach churns**
- Your body temperature heats up
- **Your feet want to kick or stomp**

There's some good news and bad news about anger. First the bad news (to get it out of the way): Anger can stay with you for a very, very, *very* long time. This may be hard to believe, but some of the adults you know and talk to every day are still angry about stuff that happened when they were kids. Because they never dealt with their anger, it just stuck around like a bad smell. You probably don't want this to happen to you.

Now for the good news: You have the power to overpower your anger!

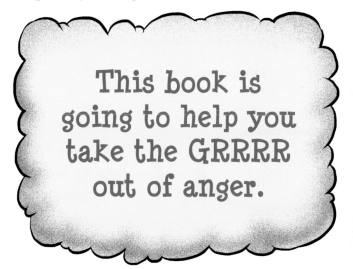

This book is going to help you take the GRRRR out of anger.

If you learn to handle your anger, you'll feel calmer and more peaceful. This can make it easier for you to get along at home, at school, and out in the world. Your family and friends will respect how well you handle your feelings. Best of all, you'll feel better about yourself. You'll be a stronger, healthier person—guaranteed.

Chapter 1

How It Feels to Be Angry

How do you know when you're angry? Some kids describe the feeling like this:

> I just get so TENSE!

> I want to take it out on somebody.

> I want the world to get away from me.

> My hands start to shake.

> It's like my heart is beating out of control.

Everything inside me is jumpy, like it has to get out!

I just want to break something.

It feels like my stomach is tied up in knots.

I feel so mad that my head could explode.

If you were to make a sound while angry, it would probably be a

grrrrowl.

Do you feel angry a lot of the time? What if you had a special thermometer that could read your anger level all day long? How high would the level go? How often would it reach the hot zones?

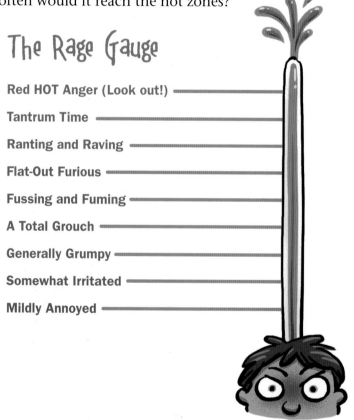

The Rage Gauge

Red HOT Anger (Look out!)

Tantrum Time

Ranting and Raving

Flat-Out Furious

Fussing and Fuming

A Total Grouch

Generally Grumpy

Somewhat Irritated

Mildly Annoyed

Maybe you don't get angry very often. That's great! But you still might want to figure out ways to deal with anger when it happens. Check out pages 33–45, "Five Steps to Taming That Temper."

On the other hand, maybe you're one of those people who practically wakes up angry. Is your mood so bad it could clear a room?

Or maybe it seems like other people are always doing things that make you mad. Then you may find yourself thinking—or saying—some pretty nasty things.

Like . . .

If your sister leaves the bedroom looking less than perfect:

Or . . .

If somebody gets a better grade than you:

Or . . .

If your friend keeps interrupting when you're trying to talk:

Or . . .

If someone accidentally bumps into you on the way to class:

Sure, other people may sometimes try to make you mad on purpose. But often they're just being themselves, or kidding around, or making mistakes. They may not even know they're angering you.

How do you feel when you're thinking angry thoughts or saying angry words?

Chances are, you feel . . .

Did you know that even just making an angry face may make you feel mad? Scientists have done studies where people in one group were asked to think about a time when they were angry; in another group, the people were told to make an angry face (like a scowl). Guess what? Both groups showed the same anger response. The scientists knew this because they could measure the people's fast heartbeats and their rising body temperatures. Plus, the people said they just plain *felt* mad.

So . . .
an angry face,

angry thoughts,

and angry words

often lead to *more* angry feelings. It's that simple.

Is reading this making you mad? Do you want to know what to do right now to make the anger stop building inside you? Read Chapter 2 for some ideas.

Chapter 2

Emergency! Quick Ways to Get the Grrrr Out

Sometimes, you'll feel that anger boiling up and know you've got to take action fast. What can you do?

Get physical!

Make use of the energy that anger produces in your body. Go outside and run around. Shoot some hoops. Walk the dog. Jump rope. Dribble a soccer ball with your feet. Ride a skateboard, bike, or scooter. Do chin-ups or push-ups.

If you want to do something indoors, how about dancing fast to loud music? (Choose music that makes you feel good, not angrier.) Or what about doing 50 jumping jacks? Pick a physical activity that takes a lot of energy and is enjoyable for you. Afterward, you'll feel calmer and more ready to deal with your anger.

Avoid doing violent things like punching a door or kicking the refrigerator. Even aggressive sports like football or boxing may not be good activities for when you're angry. For many people, getting aggressive can actually increase the angry feelings.

Do something with your hands!

It may help to squeeze something with all your might. You can use a pillow, a ball, or a big clump of clay or mud. Another idea is to make two fists, and then throw open your hands—as if you were tossing your angry feelings away. Do this until you feel calmer.

Vent!

Sometimes, you just need someone who will listen to you "vent" your anger. Choose someone who will let you complain for a few minutes without interrupting. (Pick someone you're *not* mad at. Venting at the person you're angry with won't help.)

I was, like, SO mad! I couldn't believe he did that! Can you believe it?! It was TOTALLY rude! I didn't deserve to be talked to that way. AS IF! I mean, who does he think he is? I feel like I should just never speak to him again.

At times, you may be so angry that you just feel like screaming. So do it! Go outside and give a big yell. Use your voice to help release that anger.

Talk "smart" to yourself!

Use your words to calm yourself down and look at the situation in a different way. Maybe you're thinking, "I'm so mad I can't stand it!" Instead, tell yourself, "I can keep my cool," or "I can get some help here instead of getting angry."

Or ask yourself, "Is this really worth getting upset about?" Talking to yourself out loud or inside your head is a way to stay in control—and that's smart.

Calm and in control—that's me.

Adjust your attitude.

Sometimes it's what you *think* about a situation that triggers your anger. Try asking yourself, "Is there a different way to think about it so I won't feel so mad?" For example, if your mom wants you to clean up your room and you think it's unfair, you'll probably feel mad. Instead, you could tell yourself, "Most moms tell their kids to clean up their rooms—it's not a big deal." Looking at it that way, you might feel better.

Breathe!

Breathing helps you calm down because it brings oxygen to your brain. Breathe in deeply while counting:

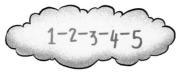

1-2-3-4-5

Let the air fill your lungs. Then breathe out slowly while counting:

5-4-3-2-1

Do this as many times as you need to, until your body and mind feel more relaxed. You might even try doing a relaxation exercise. You'll find one starting on the next page.

Relax in 10 Easy Steps

This relaxation exercise is easy to learn. Read through the steps before you give it a try.

1. Find a quiet place where you won't be disturbed. (If possible, go outdoors—to the yard or to the park, for example. The fresh air will feel good.)

2. Lie down on the grass (or on the floor). Get comfortable.

3. Close your eyes, but don't fall asleep.

4. Breathe deeply. Focus on your breath going in and out. Count to five as you breathe in; count backward from five as you breathe out. Take your time.

5. When you feel calmer, continue the deep breathing, but as you breathe out, say the word *relax* in your mind.

→

6. In time with your breathing, begin to relax your muscles from head to toe. Start with your forehead. Tense those muscles as you breathe in, and then relax them as you breathe out.

7. Continue tensing and relaxing—moving downward to your shoulders, arms, hands, stomach, legs, and feet. Each time, breathe in as you tense the muscles, and breathe out as you relax them.

8. Once you've reached your toes, take a rest. Keep breathing deeply.

9. Slowly open your eyes. You are now relaxed.

10. Enjoy this feeling!

Chapter 3
The Different Faces of Anger

Some kids treat their anger like it's front-page news. They want the *whole world* to know they're mad. They yell and scream. They kick and stomp. They pout and sulk for days.

Some kids show their anger by bullying others. Bullying is when a person *purposely* and *repeatedly* hurts or scares someone. Usually, the person doing the bullying has some kind of advantage, such as being bigger or stronger or more popular.

There are four main types of bullying:

1. Physical: When someone uses his or her *body* to scare, hurt, or control another person. This kind of bullying includes hitting, punching, tripping, kicking, blocking, pushing, or holding someone down.

2. Verbal: When someone uses *words* to hurt someone else. For example, the person spreads rumors; makes mean comments; yells, swears, or laughs at the person; or criticizes someone's appearance, family, behavior, disability, or background.

3. Relational: When bullying damages a person's *relationships* with friends or peers. It includes gossiping, spreading lies and rumors, or refusing to let someone join in. Sometimes the bullying takes the form of "the silent treatment." The person is ignored or given dirty looks and eye rolls.

4. Cyber: When someone uses a *cell phone or computer* to bully someone. For example, the person "cyberbullies" online by sending cruel messages or photos, or by ignoring someone in chats or not responding to their messages on group sites. Cyberbullying

hurts people through email, online chat sites, blogs, instant messaging, online gaming, or websites.

Bullying hurts no matter what form it takes. If you're being bullied, you probably feel angry, sad, alone, and helpless. But help is out there. See pages 24–25 for a list of people you can go to. If possible, take notes about each bullying incident so you can tell an adult exactly what happened and when. You *don't* have to find a solution to a bullying problem on your own. Please reach out for help.

Hidden Anger

Some kids try to hide their anger. They think stuffing or squashing it inside is a way to deal with it.

But you can't "smoosh" anger. What happens when you do? The anger won't stay down for long. Think of anger as a big fat beach ball. When you push it under-water, the beach ball puts up a fight. No matter how hard you try to force it down, that ball pops right out of the water. The same thing is true with anger: No matter how hard you try to force it down, it finds a way to come back up.

Kind of like throw up.

Maybe you get mad at yourself for almost any little thing you do. (For example, if you say something silly, goof up your homework, lose a race, or get the wrong answers on a test.) When things like this happen, does a mean little voice start talking in your head, saying things like . . .

When you tell yourself these things, it's like telling yourself off. The mean words inside your head can make you feel miserable. It's almost like you're punishing yourself. And you know what? You deserve to be treated better than that.

Don't be so hard on yourself. *Everyone* makes mistakes. Beating yourself up doesn't help—and neither does beating up someone else.

It's okay to be angry. Everybody gets angry sometimes. It's part of being human. You might get mad at someone else. You might get mad at yourself. Sometimes, you might even feel mad at the world.

But if you . . .

- get mad at people super fast

- break stuff when you're mad

- hurt or bully others because of your anger

- feel angry with yourself most of the time

Or

- spend your life being cranky or crabby

. . . then you need some help with your anger.

A HOT TEMPER isn't COOL.

Help Is Here

Sometimes anger takes over people's lives. What if you feel really angry or depressed all the time? Or are thinking about hurting yourself or someone else? Or are afraid someone else is going to hurt you? Get some help right away. You can:

- Talk to a grown-up you trust.

- Go to 211us.org to find a local phone number you can call to talk to someone who can help.

- Call the toll-free National Suicide Prevention Lifeline at 1-800-784-2433 (1-800-SUICIDE).

- Call the National Hopeline Network hotline 1-800-442-4673 (1-800-442-HOPE).

- Look in the Yellow Pages (yellowpages.com) and type in "Crisis Intervention."

Adults Who Can Help

Here are some adults who might be able to help you talk about anger:

- a parent

- a stepparent

- a foster parent

- a grandparent

- an aunt or an uncle

- your friend's dad or mom

- **a neighbor you know well**

- a teacher

- a counselor at school

- a coach

- **the principal**

- a doctor

- a professional counselor, psychologist, or therapist

- a leader at your place of worship

- **a social worker**

- a caregiver, like a sitter or childcare provider

- a scout or club leader

Here are some words you might try:

> I'm so mad, and I need to talk about it.

> I think I need some help with my angry feelings.

> I'm being bullied, and I need help.

Sometimes, it's easier to write your feelings in a note instead of saying them out loud:

> Dear Ms. Brown,
> I feel mad and upset a lot of the time. Can you help me with this? I really need to talk to someone. I'm writing to you because you've helped me before.
> Thank you,
> Tyler

When finding an adult, keep these two things in mind:

1. Choose someone you trust.

2. If you don't get the help you need from that person (for whatever reason), talk to someone else. Don't give up: keep looking until you find a grown-up who can help.

Chapter 4

The Dopey Things Angry People Do

Here are five true stories about things some kids have done when they were mad. (Their names aren't mentioned for privacy reasons.)

There was a girl who was almost always mad at her parents. She liked to "get even" by doing mean things behind their back. Once, she took the best photo of the whole family and tore it in half before putting it back in the frame. Another time, she threw grapes on the carpet and mashed them in with her feet. Of course, she got in more and more trouble when she did these things—and ended up angrier and angrier!

A boy and his sister used to get in lots of silly fights. They'd argue about which game to play or who got to sit in the front seat of the car. One time, the boy was so mad that he secretly stole his sister's favorite stuffed animal and gave it away to a friend of his. From then on, when he got mad that's what he'd do. The problem was, after he and his sister would make up, he didn't know how to tell her about the belongings he'd secretly given away—even when she went around looking for them. So, he kept quiet about what he'd done and then felt worse than ever.

Then there was a boy who was really into sports. He played soccer and football. Even though he loved these games, he'd get angry a lot on the field. He bossed his teammates around, and he yelled at them when they made mistakes. When he acted this way, his teammates didn't like him much. He'd get mad at himself, too, and throw the ball down hard or swear if he made a mistake. Finally, his dad took him off the teams until he could be a better sport. His dad wanted to show him that sports weren't an excuse to act tough.

Another girl had a habit of slamming her bedroom door really hard whenever she got mad. After a while, her parents got sick of it. They asked her to stop, but she refused. So the very next time she did it, her parents removed the door from its hinges. They told her she couldn't have it back until she learned a better way to handle her anger.

How do you think she felt when she got dressed every morning with no door?

Two girls who were best friends both had a crush on the same boy. This started a competition to get the boy to like them. Instead of staying friends, the girls grew apart because their anger built up. One girl started texting the boy, writing mean things about the other girl.

The other girl found out about the texts and asked the boy to show them to her.

Abby thinks she's so hot, but I know for a fact she forgets to brush her teeth. And she laughs like a donkey!

He did. The one who sent the texts tried to deny that she'd said anything bad—but the proof was right there on the screen for everyone to see.

That's the thing about angry or rude texts, emails, instant messages, and handwritten notes: you can't undo "send." Just remember: what *goes* on-screen *stays* on-screen. Forever.

It's true that anger can really make you mad. But anger is never an excuse for being mean.

What happens when you do stupid stuff when you're mad?

REGRET.

(Regret means you wish you hadn't done it, but it's too late to take it back.)

Can you think of a time when you were angry and did something you later regretted? Maybe you flew into a rage and felt bad about it afterward. Maybe you told someone off and didn't ever apologize. Maybe you hurt somebody you care about, like your friend or your pet. Maybe you ruined something that belonged to somebody else. Or maybe you ruined things for yourself.

Angry behavior doesn't solve problems. Most times, it makes things worse.

If you recently did something you regret and you feel a need to apologize, go ahead and do it. Just say, "I'm really sorry. Can you forgive me?" You and the other person both may feel better.

 If you feel shy about doing this face-to-face, you could send an "I'm sorry" note instead. Or you could send an email or instant message.

Chapter 5

Five Steps to Taming That Temper

If there's one positive thing about anger, it would have to be that it gives you extra energy. But that very same energy can make you feel like you're ready to fight or explode. So, what are you supposed to do with all that energy?

You can turn it into POSITIVE POWER.
How? The place to start is by

TAMING THAT TEMPER.

You've got the power to cut it down to size.

First, you need to *cool* down so you can *calm* down. Doing this will put you back in control. Check out Chapter 2 for quick tips on cooling down.

Once you're calm, you should be ready to tame your temper. To make it easier, try it in steps, like these:

STEP 1

Know what pushes your "anger buttons."

You probably could name a few things you've gotten angry about. Maybe the list is pretty long! Think of these as your anger buttons. You get mad when they're pushed.

Here are some things kids often feel angry about:

- being told to do something they don't want to do

- something that doesn't seem fair

- getting teased or pushed around

- someone taking or breaking their stuff

- not being allowed to do something they want to do

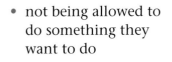

- being left out of a game or an activity

- seeing other kids cheat or tease

BEEP!

- getting bossed around

- getting criticized

- not getting enough attention

- someone making rude remarks about their race, religion, looks, or other personal stuff

- issues that affect the world, like problems with the environment, wars, acts of terror, or school shootings

It helps to know what your anger buttons are, so ask yourself about them. You may even want to write them in a list. Then, if your buttons are pushed, you can stop, take a deep breath, and pull yourself together. Just because you've gotten mad in the past doesn't mean you have to react that way now.

STEP 2
Know your body's anger "warning signs."

If you pay close attention, your body will tell you when you're getting mad.

- You may feel hotter.

- You may get shaky.

- You may feel as if your thoughts are spinning out of control.

- Your head or stomach might start to hurt.

- You may feel jumpy or helpless or ready to burst.

- You may want to yell or cry.

- You may find that you've squeezed your hands into fists.

Next time you're mad, take a moment to notice the ways your body reacts. Those are your warning signs. Think of them as your own personal "heads-up."

STEP 3
Stop and think.

Anger is a tricky emotion. You could even call it a "master of disguise." That's because anger is often a mask that hides another feeling.

Anger is sometimes a cover-up for:

- frustration
- shame
- fear
- jealousy
- sadness
- guilt
- disappointment

Why the disguise? It might be because those other feelings are hard to face or talk about. It's easier to get mad than to admit to yourself that you might be disappointed, jealous of someone, or ashamed of something you did.

Next time you get mad, stop and think about what's going on.

Ask yourself:

Here's an example:

Maybe your best friend got voted class president and is getting all sorts of attention because of it. You helped her get votes and you're glad she won, but it doesn't seem like anyone knows how much work you did to help. You feel angry whenever people come up to your friend to say "congratulations." That answers the question, **"What happened?"**

Maybe when you found out about your friend's success you felt jealous and left out—even though part of you is happy she won. You might have felt these feelings along with your anger. Or you might have felt them right before you got angry. That answers the question, **"What else did I feel when it happened?"**

Here's another example:

Suppose you were mean to your little brother and his friend. Your dad or mom found out and grounded you. That's what happened.

Maybe while you were picking on the younger kids, you felt strong and powerful. Or maybe you felt guilty or unhappy with yourself. (Being mean usually shows anger.) Then, when your parent disciplined you, you may have felt sorry about what you'd done, or disappointed about missing out on something you'd planned to do. So you got angry. Those are all the feelings you had while everything was happening.

Being able to answer those two important questions can help you understand your feelings better and figure out if you need to talk to someone about what's going on. Plus, you'll be *thinking* instead of just letting your anger build.

On the other hand, maybe you're simply

ANGRY.

Who wouldn't be mad if their sister broke their favorite video game on purpose, or if it poured rain on the day of the big soccer tournament and all the games were canceled? Even if anger is the main thing you feel, it's still a good idea to stop and think about those two questions. Doing this might make it easier for you to get to the next step.

STEP 4
Cage your rage.

Anger is a strong emotion. But YOU are *stronger*. You have a choice about how to handle yourself. It takes a strong person to make the right choice. You can do it!

If you start to feel angry, don't lash out or swear your head off. Instead, walk away from whoever or whatever is making you mad, if this is possible. If you're angry with a teacher, a parent, or another adult, you might first say, "I need a few moments to pull myself together" or "I need a minute to calm down." If you're mad at a friend, you can say the same things. Or, you could just say you need to take a break for a moment. Head to the nearest bathroom and splash your face with cool water. Get a drink of water, too. (Quick ways to cool down.)

Take a few deep breaths to help yourself think more clearly. Remind yourself:

"I have the power to overpower my anger."

If you want to *really* relax, try the exercise on pages 17–18.

STEP 5
Decide what to do.

Once you've pulled yourself together, it's time to figure out what to do about what's making you mad. Doing something is important because it means you're taking action. The trick is, don't take a negative action, like hurting someone with your fists or your words. You want to make a good choice, not a bad one. When you make a *good* choice, you show your anger that YOU are the boss.

Here are three positive things you can do:

Talk it out. The important word here is *talk*. When you're angry, you might be tempted to yell or shout. Or you might stop talking altogether. Instead, tell somebody how you feel. You know that talking to adults can help. So can talking to friends, especially ones who are good listeners. Ask for their advice. This isn't about getting friends "on your side" *against someone else*. It's about putting your heads together to solve a problem in a healthy way.

You may decide to talk to someone you're mad at. There are positive ways to do this, too. Chapters 6 and 7 have more ideas and information on talking about anger.

Stand up for yourself. Suppose you're angry because someone insulted you. Tell the person how you feel. You might say: "I don't like what you said. I deserve more respect." Or suppose you've been treated unfairly. You could stand up for yourself like this: "This situation isn't fair. Let me tell you what really happened."

Express your feelings. Lots of people have found that writing down their feelings is one of the best ways to handle them. You could write in a journal or diary. Or you could write a rap, a song, or a poem. You might write about how you feel and what you do when you're angry, or about what you can do to change any negative "anger habits" you might have.

Maybe you'd rather express your feelings through drawing, painting, or some other kind of art. Go work with some clay or build something with a hammer and nails. You could also play an instrument or sing as a way of expressing what you're feeling.

Page 45 lists the steps for taming your temper. You can photocopy the steps (or get the online version at www.freespirit.com/grrrr) and keep them with you in your pocket or backpack. Make an extra copy to put on your bulletin board or mirror at home. It's a good reminder that you can get hold of your anger before it gets hold of you.

5 Steps to Taming That Temper

1. Know what pushes your "**anger buttons.**"

2. Know your body's anger "**warning signs.**"

3. **Stop** and **think**. Ask yourself:

"What happened that made me get angry?"

"What else did I feel when it happened?"

4. **Cage** your **rage**:

Don't lash out.

Walk away.

Take deep breaths.

5. **Decide** what to **do**.

Chapter 6

The Power of Words

When you want to express your anger, it helps to have words to describe how you're feeling. Here are some words related to anger. Can you think of others?

Anger Words

mad   ticked off   hot-headed

crabby   riled up

furious

resentful   indignant

irritated   mean   bitter   grouchy

out of control   angry

ornery   irked   cranky   powerless

annoyed   frustrated   enraged   snarly

bugged   peeved   aggressive   grumpy

hostile

Here are some words related to positive power. These are words that express how you want to feel—and how you *can* feel when you've handled anger in a positive way:

Power Words

confident   content   strong   clearheaded

safe   in control   upbeat

sure   assertive   mindful   peaceful

happy   composed   can-do   healthy   careful

assured   at ease   positive   capable

relieved

cool-headed   thoughtful   proud

Do you swear or hear a lot of cuss words at school or home? Lots of people swear when they're angry—or even when they're not. Swear words can be hurtful and embarrassing. Plus, they can make you (and others) feel even angrier. Cussing will probably get you in trouble, too.

Instead, use Anger Words to say how you feel: "I am furious about this!" Or make up your own "curse words" that aren't curse words at all. "Shiitake mushroom!" "Flammit!" "Firetruck!"

Often when you're mad at someone, you need to talk about it. Otherwise, you might get into a "blame game" where both people just get madder and madder.

"It's all YOUR fault!"

"No, it's all yours!"

"I didn't do anything!"

"You always think everyone ELSE is to blame!"

Sometimes, it seems weird to talk to someone you're angry with. You might even feel that it would be easier to fight, or freeze the person out, or slink away. But doing those things won't solve a problem. Talking face-to-face is a better way to handle the situation.

How to Use I-Messages
(and Avoid the Blame Game)

You can talk about what's happening by using "I-messages." *I-messages* are especially helpful when you're angry with someone else. They let you talk about how you feel—without blaming. Maybe inside you'd like to blame the other person. But doing so can make that person want to argue or fight back. I-messages are *positive*. They can help keep the conversation calm and respectful.

Here's how I-messages work. Suppose your brother or sister always digs around in your desk and uses your stuff.

State your **feeling**. Use the word "I" when you do this:

Say **what** it is that led you to feel this way:

Say **why** you feel this way:

State what you want to have happen to **solve** the problem:

More I-messages in action:

If it's not possible to talk to the person directly, you can make a phone call or write a note or an email using I-messages.

> Dear Kelly,
> I felt sad when you and Enrico played that joke on me because it was sort of mean. I would feel better if you would apologize.
> —Matt

With I-messages, practice is the key. At home, you can practice by doing role plays, where you and family members try out conversations like the previous ones. Do this when you're *not* angry so you can see if I-messages feel comfortable.

When using I-messages, keep your body calm like your words. Although you may want to scowl and wave your arms, *don't*—because I-messages are about keeping your cool. Relax your body, make eye contact, and put a confident expression on your face. If you can do this while speaking about your angry feelings, the other person is more likely to listen.

Your words are very powerful: they can hurt or they can help. When you use words in a positive way, you're more likely to get a positive result. And that means you're well on your way to solving an anger problem.

Chapter 7

Six Steps to Solving Anger Problems

Have you ever been mad and found yourself in a conversation like this:

"What's your PROBLEM?"

"I don't have a problem. YOU have a problem."

"Oh yeah?"

"Yeah!"

"You're such a loser."

"I know you are but what am I?"

"I know you are
but what am I?!"

"Shut up!"

"You shut up!"

"Oh yeah?"

"Yeah!"

"What's your PROBLEM?"

"I don't have a problem.
YOU have a problem."

This could go on forever. In the history of the world, a conversation like this *never* solved a problem.

If you want to have a conversation where you *really* get somewhere, you can. In fact, you can learn to resolve conflicts with other people, whether they're other kids or adults. This is another way of turning your anger into **positive power.**

Before you try to resolve a conflict with someone else, you have to make sure you're calm. First, be sure to tame your temper (see Chapter 5). Doing that should help you feel ready to deal with the problem. Then you can follow the six steps . . .

STEP 1
Get yourself ready for a talk.

Clear your mind of angry words and decide if you're REALLY ready to talk things through with the person. Take a few deep breaths if you need to. Do you feel nervous or upset about confronting the person? It's natural to feel that way. Keep in mind that talking things over is one of the best ways to solve problems. You're doing the right thing!

STEP 2
Say what the problem is.

Suppose a close friend made fun of you in front of other kids during lunch. You're mad and you feel that you can't trust your friend anymore.

Be honest as you state the problem, but stay calm and matter-of-fact. Here are some words you can use: "You made fun of me at lunch in front of everybody. Can we talk about that?"

- **If the person's answer is no,** ask about a better time. Both people have to be willing to talk for problem solving to work. If the person puts you off and won't talk, you can say:

> I'm sorry you're not willing to talk about it. I was angry when you said mean stuff in front of everyone. It was really embarrassing.

Even if you're tempted to use angry words here, don't. You can walk away knowing that you did what you could. You may need to find another friend or an adult to talk to now, especially if you're still angry or hurt.

- **If the person's answer is yes,** be honest about your feelings. You might start out with:

> I thought you were my friend. Why did you make fun of me like that? It really hurt.

The key here is to speak calmly but honestly. Try not to raise your voice.

STEP 3
Listen to the other person.

Your friend might try to explain what happened. **Be an active listener:**

- **Look** at your friend and nod when you understand.

- **Don't interrupt.**

- **Repeat** in your own words what you think the person means—to make sure you really understand. ("It sounds like you thought you were just being funny." Or, "So you weren't trying to be mean." Or, "You don't know why you did it, but you didn't mean to make me mad.")

- **Ask questions** if you don't understand something.

This isn't the time to jump in and judge or comment: just listen. The purpose here is to make sure the other person has a chance to explain or tell his or her side. This is also a time when the person might apologize. It's up to you to accept the apology, if you want to. And you'll have to decide whether you can trust the person next time.

STEP 4
Explain how you feel.

Tell the other person how you felt or feel now, and what you'd like to have happen. Use an I-message.

Try this approach:

I felt angry and hurt when you made fun of me in front of everyone, because it seems like you don't care about me or respect me. I need to know you are really my friend.

Or, try this:

When you called me a pig, I was really embarrassed. Now other people are making fun of me. I need you to be my friend and be there for me, not embarrass me.

But if it was a mistake or an accident, you might say:

> I was really mad and embarrassed that you called me a pig and made everyone laugh at me. I know you didn't mean to hurt me, and I'm not mad at you anymore. I still need to know you won't do that again, though.

STEP 5
Talk about ideas for solving the problem.

At first, just think of all the ideas you can, even if some of them seem silly. Then talk about which ideas might actually work. For example, maybe your friend promises not to do this again and you decide to give her another chance. Maybe your friend wants to talk about when it's okay to tease and when it isn't. Maybe you want your friend to tell the others that she's sorry she made fun of you and she didn't really mean it.

STEP 6
Choose an idea to try.

You might say, "Let's try that. You'll be more careful and not make fun of me in front of other people. If you think something might be funny but you aren't sure I will, you'll ask me  first before teasing me in front of other people." Also set a time to see how the idea is working.

If it's not possible to solve problems because the person doesn't want to cooperate, you'll have to decide on another approach. It might be:

- not sitting with the person at lunch any more

- no longer spending time with the person

- talking to an adult you trust about what to do

This may seem like a lot of things to think about! But once you get used to talking about problems in this way, it will become more and more natural.

If you feel more comfortable trying these ideas out by calling the person on the phone, that's okay, too. Later on, you can work your way up to talking with people face-to-face. You may want to practice first in front of the mirror so you can rehearse what you'll say.

For ideas about adults you can talk to, see pages 24–25.

You could also ask someone to *role-play* the scene with you first. A parent or a friend could pretend to be the person you're talking to. This will help you be more prepared to talk to the real person when you're ready.

Try this . . .

Here's another situation. Read through the whole situation. When you're done, go back and read it again. This time, see if you can find each of the six problem-solving steps. Give yourself a point for each step you find. Give yourself a bonus point every time you recognize I-messages. Give yourself double bonus points if you can think of other I-messages the person could use, or other solutions to the problem.

Suppose you got a video game for your birthday. You love to play it. But whenever you start to use it, your older brother arrives on the scene and wants to get in on the game. Next thing you know, he's shouting and telling you how to play—and that's the last thing you want. You feel like hollering, "Get off my back, okay?"

This is annoying and upsetting. It's like you're minding your own business, and suddenly your brother has to come along and act like the boss. Finally, you can't take it anymore. You turn off the TV, grab the game (so he can't play it either), and leave. After doing some jumps and wheelies on your bike with your friends for a while, you're calmer and ready to go back home. You think about how you can talk to your brother about your problem.

When you go inside, your brother is eating macaroni and cheese at the kitchen table. No one else is around, so you say: "I need to talk to you about what happens when I'm playing my new video game. Sometimes I just want to play it by myself, but you come in and start telling me what to do. That isn't fun for me. Is this a good time to talk about it?"

Here are some things you and your brother might say next:

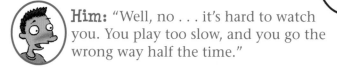

Him: "What's the big deal? I'm just watching. You don't even know how to play it right. You need all the help you can get!"

You: "So you're trying to help me?"

Him: "Well, no . . . it's hard to watch you. You play too slow, and you go the wrong way half the time."

You: "It sounds like you get frustrated watching me play."

 Him: "No kidding."

You: "I get frustrated, too, when you jump in and start yelling. It seems like you want to take over, and I just want to play it my way by myself."

 Him: "It's a cool game, and you play like a dork—I could have such a blast with that game!"

You: "Well, it's my game, and I think I should be able to play it my way. Could you at least ask me first if it's okay to watch me play?"

Him: "Yeah, whatever."

Now what? Sometimes the person you want to solve the problem with isn't all that willing to cooperate. Don't give up! At this point, you might say to your brother:

> I'd really like to solve this problem. Do you have a different idea?

Or

It sounds like you think I'm making a big deal of this. But it's important to me. Are you willing to talk about this with me?

If your brother is willing, you can talk about ideas to fix this situation. Maybe you and he can take turns every other day. Maybe you'll agree to let him play with you some of the time, but not all of the time. Maybe he'll convince you he could give you some pointers for upping your score. Or maybe he'll understand that he's been bugging you and will just agree to stop. When you really start to talk about a problem with someone, you may be surprised at some of the ideas that come up.

Once you decide to try something, you might finish up your conversation by saying something like this:

> Okay. You'll leave me alone, and I'll let you use my game once in a while. Can we try it this way till Monday and see if we're both happier?

Of course, if your brother isn't willing to talk things over, or if he just keeps bugging you and making you angrier, you'll need to find another way to deal with this problem. Maybe your mom or dad could help you figure out what to do. Maybe you can try talking with your brother again later.

Or maybe you'll see that your brother isn't going to change and you'll decide to stand up and get really close to the TV screen while you play, totally blocking his view. That way, you might both laugh and he might not butt in so much. Sometimes humor can really help change an angry situation.

There are two important things to keep in mind when it comes to solving anger problems:

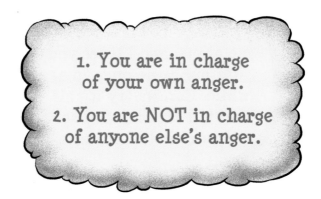

1. You are in charge of your own anger.

2. You are NOT in charge of anyone else's anger.

So don't blame yourself if the other person stays mad or won't talk things through.

When you work to solve a problem, even if the other person decides not to cooperate, you're taking charge of your anger. Give yourself an extra two points for turning your anger into **positive power!**

Page 69 lists steps for solving anger problems. You can photocopy the page (or get the online version at www.freespirit.com/grrrr) and keep it in your pocket or backpack. Make an extra copy to put on your bulletin board or mirror at home. Then you'll have a handy reference when you want to figure out how to talk through a problem with someone.

6 Steps to Solving Anger Problems

1. **Get yourself ready for a talk.**
   You want to be calm.

2. **Say what the problem is.**
   Say this in a firm but respectful way.

3. **Listen to the other person.**
   Nod; don't interrupt. Repeat back
   what you think the person means. Ask
   questions if you don't understand.

4. **Explain how you feel.**
   Use I-messages to do this.

5. **Talk about ideas for solving
   the problem.** Try to think of lots
   of good ideas.

6. **Choose an idea to try.**
   Also set a time to see how it's going.

Chapter 8

Anger Radar

Now that you know a lot about anger, you can learn to turn on your anger radar. This means you'll be able to pick up the angry "vibe" around you anytime.

It's pretty easy to tell when certain people are angry. All you have to do is look at the expression on their face. But sometimes, people try to hide their anger. They may get quiet or even have a blank look on their face. You can turn on your radar and notice some other clues about whether they might be angry.

Maybe the person:

- stops talking or gives the "silent treatment"

- swears a lot

- wants to be alone all the time

- thinks of ways to hurt other people or get revenge

- plays mean tricks or jokes on others

- thinks, talks, or writes about running away

- tries "secret" ways of showing negative feelings, like doing graffiti, damaging other people's stuff, or stealing

- tries out dangerous behaviors like smoking cigarettes, drinking alcohol, sniffing aerosol cans, using illegal drugs, or taking medications prescribed for someone else

- starts eating all the time or hardly eats anything at all

- threatens to do mean or dangerous things

- brags about having a weapon at home or in a locker

Sometimes angry people get involved in behaviors that are pretty risky. Instead of dealing with their feelings, they may try to "numb" or block them by using alcohol or other drugs. Kids who get drunk or high to cope with their problems may feel different for a little while—not necessarily better, though. And later on, they usually end up feeling just as bad or worse. Plus, kids may even think that some drugs are "safer" than others—but they're not. Some drugs that seem like a way to get away from problems can lead to serious illness and death. Even drugs prescribed by a doctor aren't safe if they weren't prescribed specifically for *you.*

Sometimes, kids who are angry will try to take out these feelings on someone who's smaller or more helpless than they are. Hitting a little kid or an animal never solves a problem. That's just being mean.

If you see someone acting in these ways, or if you've done some of these behaviors yourself, you can get some adult help. Getting help is a way to use your **positive power.** (For more on positive power, see Chapters 5 and 7.)

Sometimes people who are angry use a weapon like a knife or a gun to get back at people or to show everyone they're mad. But weapons aren't a solution. If you're this angry, or if you see someone else who is, get some help fast. Go to an adult you trust *right away.* (Run, and you'll get there faster!) Talking to someone about your feelings or your fears can really help. Even if you only *think* that someone has a gun but you don't know for sure, tell a grown-up. A grown-up can help keep you and everyone else safe.

Anger radar is useful in other ways, too. When it's turned on, you'll probably notice angry behaviors in lots of different places—places you might not have suspected. Like on TV. Or in movies. Or in video games. Or on the Internet.

It's like this: You're sitting at home quietly watching the screen. You're not angry—you're calm, you're cool, you're perfectly fine. But wait! According to experts, you may be witnessing more than 20 violent acts every hour. Things like people yelling, screaming, hitting, pushing, kicking, killing, and blowing people up. By the time you're 18, you may have seen around 200,000 acts of violence on TV.

Did you know that the American Academy of Pediatrics recommends that kids limit *all* screen time (TV, movies, computers, tablets, video games, e-readers, and phones) to two hours a day? Limiting the time you spend watching screens can help you avoid seeing too much violence. It can also keep your brain calm and working and give you time to do other things that help you feel happy and strong instead of angry.

Even if you know that what you see on TV isn't real (like cartoons and action movies), you may get more aggressive. You may feel the urge to get rough with someone. After all, you see the "good guys" roughing up the "bad guys" all the time and being called heroes for it. And in video games and gaming apps, you might even *be* the "bad guy"—the character or avatar doing the violent actions. This can make you feel more aggressive even when the game is over.

While watching violent TV shows or hearing scary stories on the news, you might also have a different reaction: fear. You may start to think the world is a bad place full of bad people. And then, if you see something violent in the real world, you might get the idea that it's "normal" or "okay." You might think violence is just a part of life. And you may think you can't do anything about it. *But you can.*

To confuse matters, you may see real people—adults you admire—acting in angry ways. For example, people at home may be angry and upset a lot of the time. (You can read more about this in Chapter 9.) This may lead you to believe that angry people are "supposed" to be loud, mean, and scary—or that it's okay to act in these ways. *But it's not.*

And sometimes, the people you see acting angry are your heroes. You may watch popular athletes, for example, yelling at each other or pushing each other around during games. You may hear stories about how their behavior isn't all that different on and off the playing field. Celebrities, too, may do aggressive things like drive fast, carry guns or other weapons, or hurt someone they love. Because you admire how a celebrity sings or performs music, or how an athlete plays sports, you may think you should admire the other ways they act. *But don't.*

SO, WHAT IN THE WORLD AM I **SUPPOSED** TO DO?!?

Here's where your anger radar can help you. Turn on your radar to be aware of when you're seeing violent stuff on TV, on YouTube, in movies, on the news, or in gaming apps and video games. Think about how you feel when you're exposed to angry or aggressive behavior. Remember those anger warning signs (page 56)? Tune in to yourself for a moment to see whether your body is sending you some signals. Feel that anger rising? Keep in mind that *you* are the one in control. With the touch of a finger, you can turn off the TV, phone, computer, or video game player. Then what?

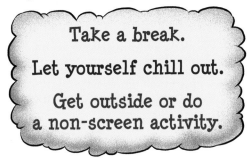

Take a break.

Let yourself chill out.

Get outside or do a non-screen activity.

And if you're upset or confused about adults you see who act angry, talk to someone about it. Let the person you're talking to know how you're feeling. Ask for some help if you need it.

You can also use your radar for one more important thing: finding a role model you can really look up to. Is there someone you admire who treats people well and shows respect for others? Someone who knows how to stay cool and calm? Someone who speaks up for herself or himself? Someone who stands for peace? Let this person be your guide for how to act and how to live.

Chapter 9

Anger
"What Ifs"

So, maybe you want to become the boss of your anger. But there are some "what if" questions getting in your way. Questions like:

"What if my parent or teacher won't help me with my anger?"

Sometimes adults aren't comfortable around anger. Maybe your dad says to you, "Don't get mad like that." Maybe your teacher says, "I don't want to hear angry words in our classroom."

When adults tell you things like this, it can seem like the adults expect you to just stop being angry. They may even make you feel like there's something wrong about feeling angry. (There's not.)

It could be that these grown-ups just aren't saying what they really mean.

When an adult says:

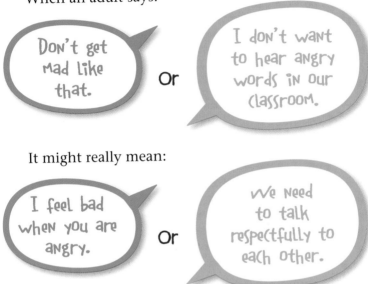

Don't get mad like that.

Or

I don't want to hear angry words in our classroom.

It might really mean:

I feel bad when you are angry.

Or

We need to talk respectfully to each other.

Try talking to your dad or teacher privately about this. You might say, "When I get angry, it seems like you think that's a bad thing. Everybody gets mad sometimes. I'm still learning how to deal with my anger. I'd like some help figuring out what to do when this happens to me."

Your dad or teacher may be glad to talk with you when you let them know you need help. If not, though, don't give up on finding a way to talk about your feelings. Talk to another adult you trust. (See pages 24–25 for a list of people to go to.)

"What if somebody is bullying me?"

Usually people who bully are angry. They think picking on other people makes them powerful. The next page has some "don'ts and do's" you can keep in mind if someone is bullying you with words . . .

DON'T ignore someone who bullies. Often, ignoring bullying makes it worse, because the person keeps trying to get you to react. He or she may just keep on teasing you or calling you names.

DO stand up for yourself. The bully probably doesn't expect you to do this. Keep your voice calm, firm, and strong. You could say, "Stop that. I don't like it." Or, "I'll report you if you don't leave me alone."

DON'T cry in front of the person who is bullying. He or she might like seeing you cry, and then bully you some more. Try to hold back the tears until later, if possible.

DO take deep breaths. Try to stay calm. Walk away and find someone to help you.

DO make sure you're surrounded by friends as often as possible. People who bully tend to target those who are alone.

Or if someone is threatening to hurt you physically…

DON'T fight back or make threats. Someone could get hurt—and besides, fighting only makes anger worse.

DO stay safe. Keep your cool and walk away. Head toward a place where there are plenty of other people. People who bully don't want to be outnumbered.

If a gang of kids chases you, or if anyone threatens you with a weapon of some kind . . .

And, remember, no matter who's bullying you, or in what way . . .

- It's not your fault.

- Making threats or fighting back won't help.

- Adults need to know what's happening so they can help you be safe. They might also be able to help the person stop the angry or dangerous behavior.

"What if an adult is angry?"

Everyone gets angry. Girls, boys, friends, brothers, sisters, cousins—even babies get angry. And, yes, adults get angry, too. This is actually very normal. Teachers, parents, coaches, club advisors, religious leaders, police officers, bus drivers, and lunch ladies get angry.

Here's another thing that's no different for adults than it is for kids: some adults handle their anger better than others.

Maybe you've seen adults act like these two people:

The teacher who led the sixth-grade orchestra had a temper. The students in his class didn't know what to do. This teacher yelled at the top of his lungs whenever he was mad. When his students' music didn't sound as nice as it was supposed to, he sometimes hit the podium so hard that he broke his conducting baton.

Once, he even threw all the music off the podium during class. This made it hard for the kids he taught to feel comfortable playing their instruments or asking questions. They never knew when he might blow up.

When an adult yells, breaks stuff, throws things, threatens, or actually hits, it isn't a healthy situation. If something like this happens to you or your friends, tell another adult about it. You might tell your mom or dad, or the principal or counselor at your school. You will be making things better for yourself. And the person you talk to might also be able to help the adult who needs to learn to handle anger in positive ways.

A boy and his mom often had good times together. When they walked the dog, or washed the dishes, or played cards, or ran errands, they would laugh and joke around. But at times the boy's mom would get *furious*. The boy was never sure when this would happen. Sometimes she would come home from work and start hollering and storming around the room. Once when they were riding in the car, she got so mad at another driver that she drove the car faster and faster, shouting at the top of her lungs. The boy was really scared. He didn't know what to do.

When family grown-ups lose control, it can be pretty frightening. It's hard to feel safe when the adults who make the rules and are in charge of you act in ways like this.

If something like this happens to you, you need an adult's help. Ask another grown-up—someone you trust—to help you figure out what to do. Together, you may decide to find a quiet, calm time to talk with the person who gets so angry.

You could say, "I really like when we get along, but I get scared when you yell and pound the table. I wish you would be more calm when you feel angry."

Remember, if someone is hitting you or hurting you, it's not okay. You can get help by talking to a trusted adult. See the list of adults you can go to on pages 24–25.

"What if I don't feel safe?"

Safety is the most important thing of all. For you, it's Job #1. So, if you don't feel safe—if you worry that saying something now could mean an adult gets even more angry with you later—get help.

If there's yelling or fighting in your home, you can help keep yourself safe. You can:

Plan ahead. Think about a safe place you can go to when the yelling or fighting starts. Go to that place and do something calming. You might read, or write in a notebook, or play a game, or listen quietly to music. If you have a cell phone, you might call a relative (like your grandpa or your aunt), or a good friend, and talk quietly.

Call 911. If you don't feel safe anywhere at home, call 911. Explain to the person who answers the phone that there is a fight in your home and you don't feel safe.

Talk to a trusted grown-up. Find an adult who can figure out how to help you be safe at home. Talk to that person about what's going on.

Page 24 has more information about how to get some help.

Chapter 10

Grrrreat Ways to Keep Your Cool

Congratulations! You've learned lots of ways to become the boss of your own anger! There are also things you can do every day to take care of yourself and handle your feelings in positive ways.

Be good to your body.

Get some exercise every day so you feel healthy and strong. Physical activity improves your mood and is a good way to use the energy you feel when you're angry.

Eat right.

It's important to eat nutritious foods like fruits and vegetables throughout the day. Avoid too many junk foods like candy and chips, which can give you the "blahs." (They're tasty when you're eating them, but they make you feel not-so-good afterward.)

Don't skip meals.

Have you ever noticed that you get a short temper if you're hungry? It's hard to feel balanced when you skip breakfast or go to practice on an empty stomach. Eating regular meals and snacks will help keep bad moods at bay.

Cut down on caffeine.

Drinking a lot of sugary, caffeinated soda can leave you feeling jumpy and jittery. Coffee drinks and energy drinks can do this, too. And when you feel that way, it's easier to get mad at little things. Plus, when the sugar and caffeine wear off, you can end up feeling tired and cranky. Try water or fruit juice instead.

Don't skimp on sleep.

Staying up late to read, watch TV or videos, or text with friends may seem like fun, but you might be a real grump the next day. Get a good night's rest every night, and even take naps if you need to.

Learn to relax.

Relaxation isn't about lying around or spacing out in front of the TV. Actually, relaxation takes some skill and concentration. It's a way to clear your mind and relax your muscles from head to toe. There's a relaxation exercise on pages 17–18 that you can learn to do. Once you know the steps by heart, you can relax anywhere, anytime.

Find fun distractions.

What's your favorite hobby or activity? Don't have one? Then get one! Maybe you could start a collection, learn a new skill, or join a club. If you already have a hobby or an activity you love, turn to it when you're having a bad day. It helps get your mind off your problems.

Know your feelings.

Try to figure out if you're actually angry, or if you might be feeling jealous, sad, frustrated, or some other emotion. When you know how you feel and why, you can better figure out how to cope.

Talk with somebody.

Whenever something's bothering you, get it off your chest. Find someone to talk to. Tell the person what you're feeling and why. That person can be an adult you trust or a good friend. If you and your friends aren't used to sharing your feelings, you may need to be the first one to try it. Chances are, your friends will be glad you opened up to them and will feel more comfortable talking about their problems, too.

Write about your feelings.

Keep a private journal for storing all your thoughts. Write in it whether you're angry or happy. It's fun and helpful to record your words on paper. You can use a notebook or special journaling book for this. Keep your journal in a private place if you're afraid someone will peek. You can also keep a journal on your tablet, computer, or phone. If you do this, get help setting up your journal from someone you trust so you can be sure what you type in will not be shared with anyone else. It's important that you *don't* journal on the Internet—nothing you write there is ever really private.

Try yoga.

Yoga combines exercise, good breathing, and learning to focus your brain. With yoga, you learn body poses like Downward Facing Dog, Rabbit, Warrior, or Spider. You hold a pose while you breathe deeply and focus your mind. Your body and mind both get to stretch and relax! Doing yoga a few times a week can help you feel calmer and less angry much of the time.

Find a quiet place.

This place can be your own bedroom or a private area of a bedroom you share with someone else. Your quiet place could be your bed or a closet—wherever you can go to feel safe and peaceful. Use this as your thinking and feeling place. Anytime you feel strong emotions and you want to be alone, go to this place to feel better.

Get into music or art.

There are two great things about music: When it's fast, it can help you release pent-up energy. When it's slow and soothing, it can help you feel more calm. Use music to help you with your emotions. You can use art to do that, too. When you're upset, it feels good to scribble, rock out with a guitar, get your hands in some paint, or mold a big hunk of clay.

Make good decisions about what you see and hear.

There's a lot of violent stuff on TV, on YouTube, in movies, and in video games and apps—even ones that are specially made for kids. Watching and hearing violent, angry stuff might leave you feeling violent and angry yourself. You can make good choices about the shows, websites, and games you view.

Help start an anger-management group.

Talk to your teacher, school counselor, scout or club leader, or someone at your place of worship about starting a group for people who want to learn to handle anger in **positive** ways.

Choose friends who help you feel good.

Are you hanging around kids who act angry and tough? Do your friends tease you or do other things that leave you feeling bad about yourself? Real friends care about you. They want you to feel good about who you are and the things you do. Look for **real friends**—ones who can help you feel happy and peaceful.

Get and give hugs.

Hugs from people you love or care about are a great way to feel a little better when you're sad, upset, or angry. You can help someone else feel better by giving that person a hug, too. (Just be sure the person wants the hug.) Hugs aren't only for times when you feel bad, either. They're a nice way to show when you're happy!

Learn to forgive and forget.

You probably know that holding a grudge against someone doesn't make life easier. And it never feels good to have a lot of fights at home or lose a friend because you argue too much. Learn to say you're sorry, and don't wait forever to get the words out. Never give an apology like this: "I'm sorry—but you sure acted like a jerk!" (The person won't feel better.) Just say you're sorry for your part in things: "I apologize for how I acted. It was disrespectful."

The other side of apologizing is forgiving. If you feel like you can do it, forgive someone who's angered you—whether that person has said sorry or not. This is a great way to put an angry moment behind you.

If you learn now how to tame your temper and use your anger in a positive way, you'll have a much easier time getting along with people. It's true! Plus, you'll grow up to be a happier, healthier adult. Someday, you just might thank yourself for learning to show your anger who's the boss.

(That would be you.)

On page 98 is a pledge to help you work on dealing with your anger. You can photocopy the page and take the pledge. (You can also get the online version at www.freespirit.com/grrrr.) Sign your name and write down the date. Ask a trusted adult to watch you take this pledge and to help you keep it. Any time you start to have trouble with your anger, look at the promises you've made to yourself. You may be inspired to keep them!

Anger Pledge

I PROMISE to work on handling my anger in positive ways.

I PROMISE to treat others with kindness and respect.

I PROMISE to treat myself with kindness and respect, too.

Name:

Date:

A Message to Parents and Teachers

Anger is part of the human condition. It's as normal as joy, sorrow, excitement, fear, or contentment. Yet, as a parent or teacher, it's hard not to be concerned about the aggressive and sometimes violent ways children—and adults—express anger.

For most people, anger is an especially difficult emotion to deal with. It's a complex feeling, closely linked to other emotions including guilt, jealousy, grief, frustration, worry, and fear. Further complicating anger is the way many of us learned to handle it ourselves. We may have understood from an early age that anger was unacceptable. We may have learned only negative ways to express and cope with it: perhaps by ignoring it (or those who make us angry), keeping an unsettled or stormy mood, lashing out with words, yelling, or hitting. Taking their cues from the adults in their lives, our children may be learning to handle anger in similar ways.

Psychologists tell us that it can be helpful to think about anger as a kind of survival emotion. If a child is angry, it's a signal. The signal might alert us that the child needs to overcome something developmentally (such as being accepted by peers, learning to compete, or mastering skills in school). It might let us know that the child needs to deal with stresses that occur in relationships (such as teasing, unfair treatment, or feeling pressured). Or it could be a sign that she or he is struggling with self-doubt, low self-esteem, or feelings of powerlessness.

Many times, children get messages from parents and teachers—often unintentional messages—that anger is bad. It can be almost an automatic response to say, "Don't get angry" or "Quit being so mad." Yet children do get angry, and so this message doesn't help them understand or work through the anger that they're experiencing. Often, too, adults tell kids, "It's okay to be angry, but it's not okay to yell (hit, kick, throw things)." This is a positive message, as far as it goes. But children need more than this. They need to:

- have ways to release angry feelings when they want to explode or strike out

- understand why they are angry

- be able to express their angry feelings, share them with others, and talk about them

- learn how to deal with the situations that lead to anger

- find ways that they can manage angry feelings

Besides handling their own anger, kids need to know what to do when other people are angry. Seeing adults or other young people seethe with anger, lose control, or shut people out is frightening for children.

We wrote this book to give kids practical strategies for dealing with angry feelings in healthy ways. You might want to read the book yourself before sharing it with your child. If you like, read it with your child or class. Talk about the ideas in it. Ask "what if" questions about some of the situations the book depicts and about situations your child or students experience. Help children plan how to avoid conflict, calm down when angry, release and express angry feelings, resolve problems with other people, and get help from trusted adults when needed. Planning ahead puts children in control and gives them positive power over anger.

Ideas for Helping Kids Deal with Anger

Here are some other suggestions for supporting children as they learn to manage anger.

Make it a point to deal with your own anger in positive ways.

If you're in a power struggle with your child, exit the scene until you can calm down. It's okay to say, "I'm too angry to talk about this right now. We'll talk later when I'm calmer." Then, when you talk, discuss what happened in a nonblaming way. Notice your own anger buttons, warning signs, and responses. You might want to ask a partner or friend to give you some feedback about what the person observes regarding how you respond to anger. If you find that you're struggling with managing your anger, get professional help.

Model appropriate ways to handle anger.
Tell your child what you're doing: "I'm feeling angry right now, so I'm going to take a walk and calm myself down." "I'm mad about something that happened at work today. I'm going to call my friend and tell him about it. Talking things through helps me figure out what to do."

Make it a goal not to argue heatedly with your partner in front of your children.
Children are very sensitive to how their parents or caregivers treat each other during arguments. They feel torn when the people they love most are fighting—especially when loud arguments or other angry behaviors are taking place. If you yell and shout at each other in front of your children, they may become angry, frightened, and upset. They may feel as if they are to blame or must somehow act as mediators. Avoid putting a child in this difficult situation by doing all that you can not to argue this way in your home. Choose a time when you can talk with your partner, calmly, behind closed doors. The point isn't for you and your partner to try to be superhuman here, but to minimize the negative or intense adult situations your kids see and hear at home.

Set reasonable rules at home.
Think of the goal of discipline as self-discipline; set clear and logical consequences that help children control themselves and get along with others. If you typically

use spanking as a form of discipline, think about the message it sends to kids: that hitting is a way to solve problems. Decide whether this is the message you're really trying to send and what other methods might work better. (See pages 110–116, for helpful resources on discipline.)

Know the signs that a child needs help with anger.

These include:

- recurring behavior problems or misbehavior that isn't typical
- sleep problems
- changes in eating habits
- unhappiness the child can't explain
- physical outbursts like slamming doors, kicking furniture, or intentionally breaking things
- ongoing irritability
- harming other people or animals
- fighting at home or at school

When children are angry, try to discover the reason.

Invite conversation when everyone is calm. Listen carefully. Avoid shaming your child for being or acting angry—even when the actions aren't acceptable. Once you know the reason for the anger, find ways to help solve the problem.

Help children learn anger-management skills.
Many kids yell, fight, swear, or throw tantrums because they simply don't know another way to show how they're feeling. Teach them words for strong emotions, so they can understand and clearly express powerful feelings. Help them find ways to calm down and gain control of themselves, and to talk things through with you and others. It can be helpful to role-play situations where anger and conflicts might occur, and have kids enact different approaches to the problems.

Let children know you expect them to manage conflicts in respectful, constructive ways.
Give them a chance to handle an angry situation on their own. If they need help, ask for their ideas about what to do. Suggest some solutions if necessary. You might also talk to the principal or guidance counselor about starting an anger-management group for kids at school.

Keep the lines of communication open between home and school.
If you're a parent, talk with the teacher about concerns you have and about how you're helping your child manage anger at home. If you're a teacher, tell parents what issues are arising for children at school. Let parents know that you are teaching kids positive ways to deal with anger, and enlist their support at home. When parents and teachers work together to help kids handle anger, children get consistent messages and guidance.

Monitor all the screens children interact with.
These include TV, movies, YouTube and other websites, video games, gaming apps, social media, email, and texting. Talk about violence in the media and how it can contribute to angry feelings and make people feel that violence and cruelty are normal or fun. Make an effort to spend "media-free" time with children playing board games, riding bikes, going to the park, or fixing meals together.

For kids with special needs, provide added support.
Kids on the autism spectrum and those with ADHD, learning disabilities, and cognitive or behavior disorders often have a low threshold for frustration and impulsivity. Teach your child social skills, and anticipate possible trigger situations so you can set the child up for success in daily interactions. Know and watch for the signals your child shows when anger is building. For many kids with special needs, meltdowns are a part of life, so be prepared to deal with them. It's a good idea to make an action plan for coping with angry outbursts at home, at school, and in other public places. Seek guidance from a child psychologist or counselor who understands the child's diagnosis and needs.

Get outside help if it's needed.
If the suggestions in this book and in the other resources on pages 107–116 don't seem to be helping, seek professional help for your child. You might ask

the school guidance counselor, psychologist, or social worker for help or for recommendations of therapists, child behavior specialists, or family counselors. You might also ask a trusted doctor or member of the clergy, or check the online Yellow Pages under Mental Health Services or Child Care Resources and Referral. If cost is a concern, let the counselor or agency know. Low-cost, graduated-scale, and free services are often available.

Unpleasant as it is, anger can actually be a positive force, helping kids stand up for themselves when things don't seem right or fair. Giving children the confidence and skills they need to cope with anger is empowering. It offers kids hope, security, and self-confidence—a chance to end the cycle of unresolved anger and lead more peaceful and constructive lives.

Resources for Kids

Books

Bullying Is a Pain in the Brain by Trevor Romain (Minneapolis: Free Spirit Publishing, 2016). If someone's bullying you, this book has practical tips and suggestions for becoming "Bully-Proof." It can also help you if you're the one who's doing the bullying.

Don't Be a Menace on Sundays! The Children's Anti-Violence Book by Adolph Moser, Ed.D. (Kansas City, MO: Landmark Editions, 2002). Here's a book that talks about all the violence you see and hear about on TV, in movies, in video games, and in your own school and community. You'll find helpful ideas for tuning out and turning away from violence and for staying safe and out of trouble.

Don't Rant and Rave on Wednesdays! by Adolph Moser, Ed.D. (Kansas City, MO: Landmark Editions, 1994). This colorful book offers ideas to help you feel mad less often. It also has tips for calming down, expressing your emotions, and controlling angry feelings.

Hot Stuff to Help Kids Chill Out: The Anger Management Book by Jerry Wilde (Richmond, IN: LGR Publishing, 1997). *Hot Stuff* teaches you how to think through your anger and calm down before you do something you might regret. With writing exercises and example situations, this book is a fun, helpful read.

Sometimes I Like to Fight, But I Don't Do It Much Anymore by Lawrence E. Shapiro (Plainview, NY: Childswork/ Childsplay, 1995). Douglas has always liked to fight, but fighting gets him in trouble with his friends and the principal. He learns to control his fighting with help from a counselor and a friendship group at school. If your library doesn't have this book, your parent or school can order it by calling 1-800-962-1141 or going to www.childswork.com.

Stick Up for Yourself! Every Kid's Guide to Personal Power and Positive Self-Esteem by Gershen Kaufman, Ph.D., Lev Raphael, Ph.D., and Pamela Espeland (Minneapolis: Free Spirit Publishing, 1999). Simple words and real-life examples show how you can stick up for yourself with other kids (including bullies and teasers), big sisters and brothers, and grown-ups, too. This book also has ideas to help you manage anger, grow a "feelings vocabulary," and solve problems.

What to Do When Your Temper Flares: A Kid's Guide to Overcoming Problems with Anger by Dawn Huebner, Ph.D. (Washington, DC: Magination Press, 2007). You can draw and write all over this interactive book at the same you learn to control angry thoughts and cool down when your temper flares.

Websites

CDC: BAM! Body and Mind
www.cdc.gov/bam
This website has plenty of activities, games, and information to help you live a healthy life. For more specific information on dealing with anger, click on the "Your Life" section, then visit the "Guide to Getting Along" to read "Iron Out Your Issues" and "Break the Anger Chain." Also, explore the rest of the website for tips on managing stress, bullying, and more.

KidsHealth
www.kidshealth.org
This site has great information on all kinds of issues related to being and feeling healthy. Enter the kids' section and click on "Feelings" to find links to information about school concerns, getting along with your family and friends, understanding emotions and behaviors, and dealing with thoughts and feelings. To learn more about handling angry situations and feelings, within the "Feelings" section click on "My Emotions & Behaviors" to check out "Taking Charge of Anger," "Dealing with Bullies," and "What Should I Do If My Family Fights?" Click on "My Thoughts & Feelings" to read "Talking About Your Feelings."

Resources for Parents and Teachers

Books and Activities

The Anger Solution Board Game. This therapeutic game helps elementary-age children learn to control their behavioral responses to anger. As players move around the board, they face various decisions and learn to make constructive choices. The game can be played by two to six players. Available from Childswork/Childsplay, 1-800-962-1141 or www.childswork.com.

The Anger Workbook for Teens: Activities to Help You Deal with Anger and Frustration by Raychelle Cassada Lohmann, M.S., LPC (Oakland, CA: Instant Help, 2010). Intended for teens, this workbook may be helpful with children ages 11 and up. It includes 42 activities and exercises to help tweens and teens look at what makes them angry, learn to communicate feelings more effectively, and develop coping skills for handling anger-provoking situations in healthy ways. (See *Cool, Calm, and Confident* on page 111 for a workbook to use with younger kids.)

The Angry Child: Regaining Control When Your Child Is Out of Control by Dr. Tim Murphy and Loriann Hoff Oberlin (New York: Harmony Books, 2002). When is angry too angry? This text covers the 10 characteristics of an angry child, the four stages of anger and how to cope with each, the family types most likely to produce angry children, the five "Cs" of successful parenting, commonsense strategies, and the causes and impact of attention deficit hyperactivity disorder.

Angry Children, Worried Parents: Seven Steps to Help Families Manage Anger by Sam Goldstein, Ph.D., Robert Brooks, Ph.D., and Sharon Weiss, M.Ed. (Plantation, FL: Specialty Press/A.D.D. Warehouse, 2004). This book offers a seven-step process to promote healthy anger management in children ages 4 to 14. Parents will learn strategies to help their kids cope with stress and anger, build confidence, and avoid harmful behaviors.

Cool, Calm, and Confident: A Workbook to Help Kids Learn Assertiveness Skills by Lisa M. Schab, LCSW (Oakland, CA: Instant Help, 2009). This book has simple exercises you can use with kids ages 6–10 to help them manage anger, stand up for themselves without seeming aggressive, learn to be both kind and assertive, and develop self-confidence and a positive self-image. (See *The Anger Workbook for Teens* on page 110 for a workbook to use with older kids.)

Healthy Anger: How to Help Children and Teens Manage Their Anger by Bernard Golden (New York: Oxford University Press, 2003). This book provides strategies adults can use when facing the anger of a child or teen. The focus is on creating a sense of control and understanding in the child while giving adults solutions to deal with outbursts or to stop an angry situation before it escalates.

How I Learned to Control My Temper by Debbie Pincus (Plainview, NY: Childswork/Childsplay, 1995). This is a storybook/workbook about Michael, who flies into a rage at the slightest provocation. Michael learns a variety of ways to control his temper and finds out how much better he is treated by both adults and other children when he talks things out. The activity section includes reproducible exercises that teach children to control their anger. If your library or bookstore doesn't have this book, order it from the publisher at 1-800-962-1141 or at www.childswork.com.

How to Talk So Kids Will Listen & Listen So Kids Will Talk by Adele Faber and Elaine Mazlish (New York: Scribner's, 2012). This expanded and updated 25th-anniversary edition of a classic parenting book discusses how parents can cope with children's anger and express their own without being hurtful, set firm limits and find alternatives to punishment, and resolve family conflicts peacefully.

No Kidding About Bullying: 125 Ready-to-Use Activities to Help Kids Manage Anger, Resolve Conflicts, Build Empathy, and Get Along by Naomi Drew, M.A. (Minneapolis: Free Spirit Publishing, 2010). This flexible resource gives educators, counselors, and youth leaders a diverse range of activities to help kids in grades 3–6 recognize feelings, understand and cope with anger, build empathy, resolve problems, and get along.

The Parent's Handbook: Systematic Training for Effective Parenting by Don Dinkmeyer Sr., Gary D. McKay, and Don Dinkmeyer Jr. (Fredericksburg, VA: STEP Publishers, 2007). This book teaches parents positive ways to handle power struggles with kids, a host of ways to discipline using logical consequences instead of punishment, and communication skills such as encouragement, reflective listening, and I-messages. The authors promote the idea of family meetings as a forum for talking about problems and building strong family relationships.

Taming the Dragon in Your Child: Solutions to Breaking the Cycle of Family Anger by Meg Eastman, Ph.D., with Sydney Craft Rozen (New York: John Wiley & Sons, Inc., 1994). Written for parents of kids from toddlers to teenagers, this book gives realistic, healthy, and positive ways to understand and defuse situations that trigger their children's tantrums, flare-ups, sarcasm, and arguments. It also shows parents how to recognize and break their own anger patterns, which children may be imitating. Each chapter combines specific information and advice with realistic examples of what to do in a variety of typical situations.

Temper Tamers: An Eight-Session Anger Management Pull-Out Program by Kathryn Pearson, M.S. (Verona, WI: Attainment Company, Inc., 2002). This step-by-step anger-management program is intended for use with small groups of elementary-age children. Groups use stories as the focal point for learning to recognize anger and other feelings and to think about and implement solutions for dealing with anger.

Transforming the Difficult Child by Howard Glasser and Jennifer Easley (Tucson, AZ: Nurtured Heart Publications, 1999). This book follows Howard Glasser's Nurtured Heart Approach to help parents understand children who have ADHD or exhibit other challenging behaviors. With great explanations and many relevant examples, the book guides parents through the process step by step.

A Volcano in My Tummy: Helping Children to Handle Anger by Élaine Whitehouse and Warwick Pudney (Gabriola Island, BC: New Society Publishers, 1998). Readily available through online bookstores or the library, this book for parents, teachers, and counselors provides a series of 25 lessons to help kids ages 6–15 handle anger through stories, games, worksheets, and interactive exercises with lots of real-world applications. Includes information on building kids' self-esteem, developing an anger-management program, and handling angry outbursts.

When Kids Are Mad, Not Bad: A Guide to Recognizing and Handling Your Child's Anger by Henry A. Paul, M.D. (New York: Berkley Books, 1999). This book sensitively and thoroughly addresses what makes children angry; how age, gender, and background can affect their expression of anger; the right and wrong ways to respond to angry behavior; and how to understand anger, foster healthy development, and strengthen bonds between parents and children. The book gives detailed information related to every age group from infancy to the teen years. The author also explains how a variety of behavior problems from depression and rebellion to addiction and aggression can be rooted in hidden or repressed anger.

Organizations

Committee for Children
1-800-634-4449
www.cfchildren.org
Offers information, curricula, and videos addressing violence prevention, impulse control, and conflict resolution for use in K–8 classrooms. You can also visit their website for links to fiction for children, arranged by age and grade, on topics including impulse control, anger buttons, identifying feelings, problem solving, keeping out of a fight, and more. Call, email, or write

for a list of products and services, including the revised third edition of the Second Step Violence Prevention Curriculum, and follow the Committee for Children on social media.

KidsHealth for Parents

www.kidshealth.org/parent

Visit this website to get more information on a variety of topics that can help you keep your kids healthy and safe. For resources specific to helping your child deal with anger, click on "Emotions & Behavior," then read "Taming Tempers." This section has instructions for modeling proper responses to anger and laying out ground rules that will help your child when they get angry in the future. For more tips and information, follow KidsHealth on Facebook (www.facebook.com /kidshealthparents).

Parents Anonymous

250 West First Street, Suite 250
Claremont, CA 91711
(909) 621-6184
www.parentsanonymous.org

Parents Anonymous is a well-established family strengthening program designed to help all parents find ways to manage their own anger and create a safe, nurturing home environment for their kids. Parents Anonymous groups, co-led by parents, meet in communities throughout the United States. Anyone in a parenting role can join at any time and can attend for as long as she or he wishes to. Check the website for a local 24-hour hotline.

Index

(The Place to Go for Things You Want to Know)

About the Authors and Illustrator

Elizabeth Verdick helped create the Free Spirit Publishing Laugh & Learn series and is the author of many books for children and teens. She lives in Minnesota with her husband, two children, and a houseful of pets who are still trying to figure out how to get along.

Marjorie Lisovskis has been editing books for kids, parents, and teachers for over 30 years. She has also written stories, songs, and school activities for kids of all ages. Marjorie has two grown children and three grandchildren. She and her husband live in Minneapolis.

Steve Mark is a freelance illustrator and a part-time puppeteer. He lives in Minnesota and is the father of three and the husband of one. Steve has illustrated several books in the Laugh & Learn series, including *Don't Behave Like You Live in a Cave* and *Siblings: You're Stuck with Each Other, So Stick Together*.

Free Spirit's
Laugh & Learn® Series

Solid information, a kid-centric point of view, and a sense of humor combine to make each book in our Laugh & Learn series an invaluable tool for getting through life's rough spots. *For ages 8–13. Paperback; 80–136 pp.; illust.; 5⅛" x 7"*

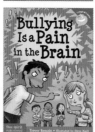

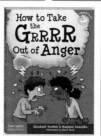

Interested in purchasing multiple quantities and receiving volume discounts?
Contact edsales@freespirit.com or call 1.800.735.7323 and ask for Education Sales.

Many Free Spirit authors are available for speaking engagements, workshops, and keynotes. Contact speakers@freespirit.com or call 1.800.735.7323.

www.freespirit.com